Vegan Pregnancy 101

Pregnancy Guide for First Time Vegan Moms and their Babies

Project Vegan

Contents

Intro

Veganism can produce amazing results by following the lifestyle yourself, or maybe seeing the positive changes in one of your friends. You probably can't wait to share the benefits of veganism with your baby. Well, you're in luck! Veganism is just as healthy for babies as it is for adults. In fact, the Academy of Nutrition and Dietics have deemed a plant-based diet is healthy at any age, including throughout infancy. Although, just like weaning your baby with any other diet, you'll need to be very strict with what you feed your baby to ensure he/she is in perfect health.

You need to be careful not to exclude nutrients only found in certain foods, and in particular, you should try to incorporate foods with vitamin D, calcium and vitamin B-12, as these nutrients are primarily only found in animal foods. Just like with any diet, it will take patience, trial and error to perfect. This book's goal is to serve as a guide for you as you are starting your journey in a society where information on vegan pregnancies is not yet so readily available.

Breaking vegan parenting myths

Here are the most common misconceptions about a vegan diet for toddlers. Remember that you will need to adjust over time and each baby's dietary needs are unique, so make sure you educate yourself as much as possible on what will work best for your little one.

Myth 1: Your body needs milk and dairy to build strong bones.

It is a fact that milk contains calcium; however, the reason for this is because a cow's diet consists of corn and soy that is fortified with calcium. As a vegan, you can get calcium straight from the source simply by eating plant-based foods that are calcium rich (such as dark leaf greens or soy based foods). As a result, you will also avoid the excessively bad fats, as well as cholesterol, antibiotics and hormones included in dairy. Take note also that Vitamin D aids your body in breaking down calcium, so be diligent on making sure your baby gets around 10 minutes of daily sunshine. On cloudy days, you can take a Vitamin D multi-vitamin.

Myth 2: Children need meat, fish or poultry to build strong muscles.

"Where will you get your protein?" is probably one of the most repetitive and annoying questions people ask vegans on a daily basis. But keep in mind no matter how irritating this can be, the question merits a cohesive reply and attention as misinformation on topics like this have lead many people away from a vegan diet.

Requirements for protein will vary based on your little one's weight and age, but do not worry too much. As long as you include protein-rich foods such as beans, tofu, lentils, nuts and peas in most meals, your child will be as healthy as he/she can possibly be!

Myth 3: Vegan diets are dangerous for children because meeting their nutritional requirements on a daily basis is unrealistic.

You will be hard pressed to find a medical doctor who can backup such claims about a vegan diet using any real evidence. In fact, the Academy of Nutrition and Dietics has found that following a well-planned vegan diet alongside proper supplementation is very safe and beneficial to an infant's health. This is one of the top nutrition authorities in the world. How is that for a stamp of approval?

So, how do we put a plan into place? After all, it's simple to become overwhelmed by macro counting proteins or calcium grams, as well as keeping track of the calories for each stage of your baby'sdevelopment. It's best to take it step by step and try to adjust as needed in the beginning.

How you should feed a baby on a vegan diet

The first form of food a baby should have is breast milk. Some of the benefits of breast feeding babies include improving the immune system, as well as lowering risk of allergies and infection. Additionally, breast milk contains essential compounds that developing infants require, which cannot be found anywhere else, including infant formulas. If you decide to breastfeed, make sure you are getting sufficient B12, as it is essential for your baby's health when breastfeeding.

What foods you should eat while breastfeeding

Pay close attention to getting sufficient calories as well as protein everyday while breastfeeding your little one. Plant foods are so calorically diluted that you need to be sure you are not only eating until you are satiated, but also meeting your caloric needs as a breastfeeding mother. Remember, you are eating for two after all.

What nutrients are most important to Vegan Infants?

Protein: Protein is the main compound that aids in growth, so it is extremely important for your child during his/her greatest time of growth, which are the first two years. However, it must be taken in very moderate amounts, ideally through breast milk. The protein in breast milk is contained by a mere 5% of the calories. This low level of protein is not found in unrefined plant-based sources such as vegetables and starches since these foods have much bigger levels of protein, making breast milk an irreplaceable source of nutrition for infants.

Iron: Iron fortified foods such as rice cereal are a great first food for babies after they have finished breastfeeding. Aside from that, you can make your own formulas from scratch by pureéing foods like squash, yams, peas, carrots, well-cooked beans, whole grains and tofu. Most raw fruits and vegetables are also great introductory foods. And if your toddler is less than 12 months old, pureéd fruits and vegetables are especially a good choice.

Fiber: Foods high in fiber are very satiating and make children feel full before they get their daily recommended caloric intake by unrefined vegetables and starches. These foods have much higher levels of protein; for example, the protein content in sweet potatoes is 6%, beans 28%, and rice 4% respectively.

Omega 3s: During childhood, the brain is one of the fastest growing parts of the body. Plants are the only source of food that can synthesize basic essential fats in the brain (omega 3s and 6.) A common misconception is that animals are the only ones that can elongate plant-based building blocks and turn them into fats (such as DHA and EPA). However, infants are also efficient in doing the same, and no source of animal derived fats are needed to help.

What foods do babies like?

Every parent has horror stories of their toddlers having a blast at your expense by redecorating the wall, ceiling, floor or even you and your clothing! It can even be difficult to predict what your little one will like, even if he/she favored it once in the past. Just be patient and things will work themselves out; this is just part of the territory when raising a child, and you will persevere in the end. Here are some tips that will encourage your baby to eat a variety of foods and nutrients to get over being picky about what's on the plate.

Use timing to your advantage

A good time to try new foods is when your baby is most hungry. Most of the time, that is the first dish of the day, right in the morning. Try to take advantage of this moment to add in more varied and nutritious foods that your baby might otherwise reject.

Add a hint of sweetness

Humans have an ingrained liking for sweetness (hence why we have a "sweet tooth"), so mix in some sweet fruits or a sweet potato into non-sweet foods such as green vegetables and starches. But stay away from processed sugars since your baby's first food has the potential to influence their future preferences, even into adulthood. As a rule, it is best to stay away from processed sugars all together, especially overtly sweet packaged baby foods like pre-packaged juices or pureés.

Don't give up

If your baby just won't give in to certain foods, that's totally fine. Hold out on that particular food so your toddler is ready when it's time to try different, newer foods once he/she has had enough of the same old routine. Don't beat yourself up over feeding your toddler the most healthy foods possible. Keep the experience fun and relaxed, and as long as your baby sticks to a variety of wholefoods, your baby will be perfectly healthy, and you will have nothing to worry about!

Vegan breastfeeding

Always remember to hydrate and feed yourself. Moms tend to forget about caring for themselves when they're too excited and busy with their little ones. When you have to provide breast milk for baby, you'll need to add about 1,000 additional calories to your daily diet. Needless to say, a crash diet is not going to be ideal for you. To provide enough for your toddler, you need to follow a sensible, well-balanced breastfeeding diet and keep yourself hydrated with lots of water.

Signs that all's well

Your baby feeds at least every 2-3 hours or a total of at least 8 times in a day for the first 2-3 weeks.

With this frequency of feeding, he/she should also produce at least 3 stools per day, which will lighten in color to yellowy-mustard on the 5th day after their birth.

Your toddler should also be gaining about an ounce a day in weight come their 5th day after being born and through the remaining first 3 months.

Babies usually wet about 7-8 cloth diapers a day or 5-6 disposables. It is hard to tell when disposable diapers are wet since they are more absorbent. So, if you aren't sure, you can take it off and compare its weight vs. an unused disposable diaper.

Note: Wet diapers alone are not enough to tell if a baby is dehydrated. Even with the lack of milk, they will still wet a diaper. The best ways to check are still looking at the output of the stools and how well your baby is gaining weight. If they do seem to be peeing less, it doesn't do any harm to check other symptoms or check with your baby's pediatrician.

Nursing wear

You need to feel comfortable while nursing. Stress and discomfort doesn't help with your milk supply. A nursing wardrobe isn't any good without a good nursing bra or tank. You can opt to wear a regular bra that you can flip up or pull aside, but this tends to loosen them and will make you lose support faster. Nursing bras and tanks provide better support and convenience since they have special snaps, clips, or hooks that allow a section of the fabric to fold down without changing the bra's support structure.

Nursing on the Go

Don't be embarrassed to nurse in public! You have the right to do so, and every mom who breastfeeds their babies should be very proud of themselves. If you prefer some privacy while you nurse your baby in public, a nursing cover will be very useful. It keeps both you and your baby comfortable since it gives you enough privacy, while hiding your baby from visual distractions while feeding.

Staying healthy and lowering complications while pregnant

There are mothers who are "high risk" when carrying a child but not all are. This should not, therefore, intimidate you because it may mean that you will only need to be monitored closely, but not that you will have problems. However, there are mothers who experience various complications while pregnant. Some have diabetes, which may magnify in pregnancy, while some have previous preterm labor, which leads to premature birth in prior pregnancies, and others have pre-existing health conditions.

Some of the complications arising from the pregnancy and delivery of a baby include:

Morning sickness

Morning sickness can become intense in pregnancies. Although it is called morning sickness, it can happen any time with or without vomiting, but it is usually worse in the morning. Nausea and vomiting, especially first thing in the morning, is also common in some pregnant women. Usually these symptoms of morning sickness disappear by the second trimester.

Preeclampsia

Preeclampsia is Pregnancy Induced Hypertension. PIH is more not so common with mothers of singles as it is mothers of twins, but it can be either mild or severe. It will be detected when high blood pressure is measured or when there is excess protein in the urine. You should consult your healthcare professional if you notice swelling on your face, hands or feet so it can be treated early. If preeclampsia is not treated, there could be higher risks of preterm labor or premature birth.

Premature labor

When labor occurs before 37 weeks, it is known as premature labor. Discuss with your doctor any signs and prevention measures of preterm labor. If you can recognize signs of premature labor early, it can easily be prevented.

Prevention of premature labor includes

- Get enough sleep and rest, put your feet up in bed or on the couch if it is possible, take naps during the day. Sleep on your side, especially the left side to relieve the pressure on your uterus and increase blood flow.

- Attend a prenatal clinic to have your pregnancy monitored by your doctor.

- Always listen to your body language and call your doctor if you notice anything odd. Early detection is the best solution for successful treatment of preterm labor. Once premature labor has been diagnosed, you will be given medications to stop or slow down labor, antibiotics for any infections and complete or partial bed rest may help. In the worst instances, you may be admitted to hospital for treatment for induced labor or C-section.

Preterm birth

When babies are born before 37 weeks, it is known as preterm birth, but with proper care, they will grow just as fine as any other babies. Report any concerns you may have to your doctor. The doctor may induce labor or perform a C-section if there are complications so that both you and your babies are safe.

You must attend all prenatal appointments so that the doctor can detect any problems early. Discuss any complications with the doctor like swelling, spotting and pain so you can get advice and preventive treatment.

Going Home:
The early days and weeks

So, how do you make it through this tough transitional period? It is important for you and your partner to have your own space and alone time at least once a day or twice every month in the beginning, and then make more time for each other as your toddler ages and has fewer dependencies.

The Early Months:
Giving your baby the best upbringing

Motherhood is exciting, and many women can't help but imagine dressing up their little ones in cute and flamboyant clothing, take pictures with them, and have loads of bonding time. What they often forget is all the effort, time, energy, money and lifestyle changes that comes with welcoming kids into their life. The stress can really be hectic, and you'll probably find yourself screaming out at your partner since you can't scream at your baby, in order to release stress. This behavior is normal, and you should make an effort to explain the difficulty of the situation to your husband so he understands. Unfortunately, for this reason and more, marital relationships often take a hit when kids are born. Don't fear though, a kid will be worth pulling through the tribulations; it is just a reality that having a kid can put a huge tension on a relationship, especially if you are unprepared on this journey to parenthood.

Another reason many marriages experience a huge amount of stress in the first year of having a kid is babies demand a lot of energy and time. So, keeping your baby on a schedule is very important. Growing into a routine-oriented parenting habit is advisable for you to cope more easily. Setting a staggered schedule to take care of your baby, making sure he/she has your undivided attention for feeding, playtime, and prepping for naptime, and being able to have as much rest as humanly possible every day, is critical for you to be able to cope with these demands.

Adjusting to new patterns

Every baby is different and has their own sleep patterns. To cope through the night and your schedule, it's ideal to have your baby in bed at the same time every night. This will soon set your baby's body clock for changing, feeding and sleeping on schedule.

Form and follow through a bedtime routine. Babies develop habits through consistency, so develop a bedtime routine that fits you and your baby best. Bath, books or music, then bed seems to be the standard flowchart routine that works best. Make this time fun and stress-free, and it will make for great bonding time between you and your toddler.

At bedtime, you will also want to lay your baby to bed drowsy, but still awake. You don't want him/her to develop sleep crutches. It may seem sweet and harmless to rock or feed your baby to sleep, but if he/she get too used to it, they'll need you every time they wake up, including in the middle of the night. The goal of this is to train your toddler to act on their sleepiness and sleep on their own.

Coping with broken sleep patterns

Let's face it, everyone gets cranky without enough sleep, and it will be unavoidable the first few months with your baby. But there are ways for you to cope better. Take quick 15-minute power naps when you start feeling tired during the day. They're not long but they will make a huge difference with your coping and energy, and will also keep you from falling asleep accidentally. Just keep your baby in a secure place and catch some shut eye, and also make sure to set an alarm so you don't oversleep.

Remember with raising a baby, you and your partner are both at work, so the burden of broken sleep in the nights should be shared as much as possible. If needed, find a way for both of you to get a break and recover some time by asking a relative to help or even a 'night nanny' who is available to work a night-time shift for caring while you and your spouse catch up on much needed sleep.

If your baby starts bottle-feeding, you can opt to take turns as partners to handle the night care alternately. Some couples agree on shifts for the first few weeks or months, since these times demand more wake ups at night with more feeds and diaper changes. For example, one parent can nap and cover caring for the baby from 7pm till 1am while the other sleeps; then the other swaps to take the next shift from 1am to 7am while the other takes his/her turn to sleep. This way, both parents are guaranteed at least a fixed amount of sleep and a chance to recover.

Using your budget wisely for your baby

Setting up and decorating a layette and nursery for a baby can be both fun and frustrating. So, when you're shopping for the nursery, think for the long term. You'll want to buy quality fixtures and furniture that can grow with your kids.

When buying a car seat, don't go for secondhand. There are expiration dates for car seats which are printed on the bottom of the car seat. Usually, the expiration is 3-5 years after its manufacturing.

You also won't always be able to tell if the car seat has been in an accident if you buy secondhand. Safety1st.com is a recommended store when buying car seats, as they have very affordable car seats with a wide range to choose from. It can seem fun to put in extra fixtures to your baby's car seat like a head bumper, or other accessories, but these "after-market" items void the car seat's warranty. So, it is best to only use the things that came with the car seat when you bought it.

A changing table is not a necessity. Changing your baby's clothes and diapers on the floor, the bed, and the couch and other places offer the same convenience as a changing table. A changing table doesn't really offer any additional advantage. If you are certain you really want a setup like that, you can find dressers that have a built-in changing pad on top.

As a smart a mom, you will want to buy stuff that has multiple uses. Items tend to be obsolete sooner if they have only one use. Instead of a diaper pail, just buy a plastic bin or trash can that closes all the way. Then, when you're done using up dirty diapers, you can clean it and reuse it for other things like a trash can or a toy basket. The goal is to buy things you can use later for other things.

Try to avoid being impulsive when buying "things," especially for the first 2-4 weeks. Your attention and time will be focused more on feeding, sleeping, changing diapers, and calming down the crying baby. There won't be much use for toys yet during this time. You'll be surprised how much laundry your little one produces in a single day, from bibs, blankets and clothes.

Assign some little zones in your home for you and your baby. Include a feeding zone with snacks and activities for you, a napping or resting zone where you can steal some time to rest but have the baby in hearing range, a neutral activity zone where you complete some chores or tasks while still spending time with your toddler.

What you will absolutely need

Stick to cheap but smart stuff. Don't get tempted by the stuff labelled as "necessary" in Babies R Us. More than all that, your child is going to need breast milk, safety, comfort, warmth, and clean diapers.

Laying down the clothing layette

If your situation calls for doing laundry regularly, and you are not getting hand me downs, here's a basic layette list of everything you should buy for your baby.

5 to 6 soft onesies

5 to 6 one piece, pajamas

2 to 3 soft fabric sweaters

1 to 2 sets of baby boots

3 to 5 blankies

A dozen diapers of any variation

5 to 6 bibs

2 to 3 crib sheets

1 crib mattress

1 sheet to cover the changing pad

5 to 6 socks

2 to 3 warm hats

Baby Thermometers

Special baby thermometers aren't a necessity, it's just marketing fabricating a need. Even pediatricians use and say the regular digital thermometers (the same ones you use as an adult) will work just fine for babies.

The diaper bag

A bag specific just for baby diapers isn't a necessity. That and any bag just for wipes or other necessities on-the-go can be easily organized in one regular backpack, and is another thing you can be smart about with your budget.

A hands-free pumping bra

This is an instant $40 savings if you can get creative with an old sports bra. You can just cut two holes in it, and there you have it! An easy DIY, hands-free, pumping bra.

Bottle Warmer

You can use a basin or a large cup, fill it with water and place the bottles there for a few minutes.

Baby gloves

Baby socks will do just fine if you want to keep your baby from scratching themselves.

Don't feel embarrassed to ask for help. Your family and friends have growing children and are probably excited to give old stuff away.

Outing advice and essentials to have when leaving home

Going out for an adventure outdoors? You'll find that travelling with your baby will be an adventure on its own. From getting ready for the trip, to going out and being out with the baby.

You'll have to consider a lot of logistics when caring for children. You will constantly change diapers, clothes and attend any other needs. Couples tend to go anti-social when a baby arrives, as even simply going out on a date can be quite a challenge. Well, let me tell you with resounding clear confidence— you can make it happen!

Start by easing into it. Don't get all too excited and make plans for the whole day of activities every Saturday. Start by activities that take a couple of hours. It is more realistic to manage and make for time that is less likely to cause a meltdown. Overstimulated babies get easily stressed. Try winning over the easier challenges like going out for a quick trip to the grocery or farmer's market. Save the bigger ones for when you and your baby are ready. For now, avoid a whole day at the beach or an all-day out shopping at the mall. Easing into it allows you the chance to develop a system that works while understanding your baby's temperament outside the house and in the car.

When you're going out shopping with your toddler, speed is the key to success. Have a plan in mind before you go so you can get the stuff, and get out. This could mean that you won't have the luxury of comparing products or trying things on. But reviews are already available online, and you can plan ahead on what to check so you can make the most of your time. You can decide then what looks right, and remember that it all doesn't have to be in one trip. You can return what doesn't fit or doesn't work out with another trip.

It also helps a lot to know which stores have the most restrooms, and to know where they are. Then check which ones have changing tables. The best ones are the ones that have family rooms where you have more space to take care of, feed and change your baby.

It's inevitable that strangers will feel compelled to greet and touch your toddler when you are just out and trying to go through your errands. This is one of the biggest interferences when taking your baby out for a trip to the grocery store, or when running an errand. To avoid this, here are a few tips you can follow. They may seem out of character or rude depending on your personality type. But hey, no one said it was not going to be a transition, right haha?

Firstly, avoid eye contact, even from those obviously trying to talk to you. You can easily tell whom your baby has caught whose attention by listening. You will hear comments aimed at your baby, but just keep your head down or straight and carry on. Otherwise, you will have to deal with every one of them and you'll never get your shopping done. Don't attract unwarranted attention by dressing your baby up as this encourages a cuteness exhibition.

You might also find that total strangers are completely comfortable touching and talking to your baby. Some babies might even enjoy the attention, while other babies get stressed over it, so depending on your baby's personality, this can make your trip harder or easier. The simple trick is, if you want to avoid being bothered by strangers, or not have the time to entertain them, you will have to be a bit of a snob and just have to keep moving.

As you start going out with your baby all by yourself, it may feel troublesome and tedious, but going out, having fun, and enjoying yourself is what is important. Family adventures make for fond memories and are a lot of fun. They don't have to be extravagant either. It can be a picnic at your favorite park or just a short day out for breakfast or lunch. You will appreciate the experience, feel fulfilled and proud that you did it, as well as have more confidence and feel more comfortable to plan and have your next family adventure.

Essentials to Have When Leaving Home

Here are some items you should make sure you have on your outing:

- Enough diapers for the trip.
- Baby wipes.
- Part of your changing kit for when you have to change poopy bottoms and clean up a mess.
- Bottles and non-breast milk.

You can opt to bring your own cool full-sized bottles packed with their pair of clean nipples. Car bottle warmers are also available and can be helpful on a trip.

- Extra Burp clothes

In case there are accidents that get you dirty (vomit, spilled juice or milk).

- New changes of clothing

Anything can happen. Anything, so pack a couple.

- Binkies

If your baby is on a pacifier, you don't want to go in a panic and rush to the pharmacy store. Keep a pacifier holder; it's just a little box that snaps close, and attach it to your baby bag. Of course, always pack a spare. Your baby can throw them and drop them and even lose them, so be ready rather than sorry.

- Baby food and snacks

Pack enough for a meal plus extra in case any of it spills, and bring about 1-2 spoons so you have extra if any of it drops, and there is no sink near you to rinse it.

- 2 bibs (for each baby)
- Washcloths
- Hand sanitizer
  A mom's best friend.

If it's hot, like in Spring or Summer:

- Sunscreen
- A cooler bag with juice
- Sun hats if applicable

If it's Winter:

- Scarfs and Warmers
- Warm Hats
- Mittens

Alternatives to outings with a baby

The World Wide Web gives you access to many things, including grocery shopping. A click of the mouse can get you diapers, non-dairy milk, groceries, and clothing (both for your little one and yourself). Still, you don't want to go into hermit mode and just hide in the house, as sunlight and Vitamin c are essential for good health, so you should still go out with your baby occasionally. Online access can be your breakaway, but there will still be a lot of occasions for bonding with your little ones, so don't worry and get clicking.

Wonderful fun at home

A warm bath is a pleasure any time of the day. You can have some fun with your baby at the tub, and he/she can enjoy getting all cleaned up too. Of course, you'll still want to supervise your baby's safety in the tub, but you'll love seeing your toddler having so much fun you might even jump in!

The messy mixes

Messy is fun! Even experts say that exposing your baby to this form of play is good for their brain development. All the ingredients you need for this recipe of fun is just around the house. Innocent messy projects will keep your little one busy and entertained for hours. Get those little hands into some finger painting; your baby will love it!

Seeking support

Having a good doctor for your baby is something that is very important to any parent. The doctor will be there for your baby from the moment of birth and as the baby grows. Regular checkups with the pediatrician will start frequently at younger ages, and become less frequent as your baby grows into a kid.

Given how important a pediatrician's support is to your baby, how do you pick the right one? You can ask for recommendations from family and friends who also have children, or you can reach out to your family doctor or even the obstetrician taking care of you during pregnancy.

Running short of recommendations?

If you ever find that you aren't getting any recommendations, as sometimes even family or friends don't like the pediatricians they've consulted, you can also look for recommendations online. There are sites that provide a list of doctors in your area, like the American Academy of Pediatrics, or even Yelp.

The important questions you should think about when choosing a pediatrician are:

- Consideri your baby's gender. Will you want him/her to be seen by a female or male doctor?
- What is the reputation of this doctor?
- Is your doctor addressing you as parents or does he/she talk to your toddler as well?
- Is the clinic staff helpful and pleasant?
- Is the clinic's location convenient and accessible to you?
- Are the doctor's services covered by health insurance?

The bottom line

Your personal experience and impressions are important when choosing a doctor, so don't ignore them. It is also important that your personality is compatible with your doctor to avoid any conflict. The pediatrician you choose will be sharing involvement in your child's life and growth, so you will want someone you can both trust and respects you as a parent.

Toddler Safety

You've probably heard of baby proofing. It is best to have carpeted floors throughout your home. Having a walk-through baby gate at the top of any staircase is a necessity for safety. Don't get too comfortable thinking your baby will stick to stuffed animals, toy boxes, or other distractions you keep in the house. Your baby will love to explore and go outside to what is unknown. You can be sure your little one will go looking for trouble when exploring.

Choose the right spot in the room. That means a spot away from anything they can pull or grab and anything that easily breaks. This includes blind cords, curtains and draperies, windows, desk lamps, wall or floor lamps, radiators, and electrical sockets.

You want to avoid the risk of your baby getting trapped between the bed and the wall. So, you can either build the rails on both sides or leave enough space on both sides of the bed while making sure the headboard is flat against the wall.

You should also place cushions for any falls from the bed like a soft rug, pillows or a sleeping bag. Also as important is that there are no loose joints, screws or other parts of the hardware, so check this regularly.

Got a crib-climbing toddler? Get a sleep sack

When your baby starts reaching mobility milestones (from crawling, standing, to walking on two feet) early, you'll find that him/her will want to start exploring more and try to escape the crib. Opting for a sleep sack, in this case, could be ideal for your toddler. Sleep sacks leave enough space for your baby to move comfortably, while keeping your babies legs and feet enclosed. This negates him/her the mobility to climb. Minimal restrictions like this could be enough to keep your baby from doing any climbing in the middle of the night.

Baby speech development and delay

Don't get tempted to use "baby talk" no matter how cute you think it is. And when you hear your toddler speak mispronounced words, repeat it back with the correct word, while emphasizing the sounds in the words. Now, don't expect that your baby can immediately perfect it, and instead praise your baby for trying so as to not cause discouragement. Your role is to teach what is correct, so it registers that way. If all you use around your toddler is baby talk, that's all he/she will learn to use, and it may be cute now, but it won't be when he/she grows to be 4 years old and every other kid their age is speaking better.

So, how can you encourage your baby's speech development to improve? Here are some language milestones to monitor:

Between 12-24 months

- Use a combination of two simple words
- Can use a vocabulary of 10 – 20 words
- Imitate some animal sounds if you like
- Wave their hands good-bye

Notes: A lot of Health Services Programs specific for Speech and Language are also available for free.

- Get your little one to copy your sounds and actions. You can help by making it fun with action songs like "Pat-A-Cake," "Itsy Bitsy Spider" and "Wheels on the Bus," and other games like clapping your hands, making rocket ships sounds, blowing kisses or "Peek-A-Boo."

Other things you can do to encourage language development include:

- For at least 30 minutes every day, give your baby the chance to listen to other noises around him/her by turning off the TV and radio. You can use this to explain the sounds your baby is hearing, like the car, or dogs barking, the birds or even the washing machine.

- Your baby will experiment with different sounds as he/she tries to play with their mouth and vocal skills to learn to speak. Listen and respond as they do.

- Use your toddler's name with eye contact, and spend time conversing with each of your children individually every day.

- Encourage members of the family, older siblings, and friends to have one-on-one conversations with your baby in the same way.

Keep in mind that you are the best person to help your baby develop. And since you have your little one and yourself, you're an established language duo and you are the best suited speech coach!

Diapering for your toddler

Assign and set up your designated changing space specific for nappy changes in the house. Everything you will be using for changing diapers should be within arm's reach, including diaper rash cream, wipes and baby powder. There should never be any reason for you to leave your baby on a changing table just to grab something. Not even for a second! Always fasten the belt and have a good grip of your baby to avoid any falls.

Choosing the right diapers

There's definitely no way around it. Until your baby reaches the potty trained stage, you will have to deal with diapers, and lots of them! Like any other parent, you will have to make the decision on what diaper to use, cloth, disposable, and what brand?

To start, there's no big difference when choosing between brands. And be it cloth or disposable, your baby will get rashes and feel uncomfortable if you leave them wearing a soiled diaper for long. Though disposable diapers have some benefits, like having moisturizer and being breathable, some babies tend to be allergic or easily irritated by the chemicals that make them absorbent. Some babies seem to prefer the comfort of soft cloth diapers the most.

Prices

Typically, you'll find yourself spending between $2000 and $3000 on disposable diapers for a single baby. If you opt for cloth diapers and accessories, the cost would be around $800 to $1000 if you do the laundry yourself. If you have them washed through a cloth diaper laundering service, the cost comes close to buying disposable diapers ranging from $2500 to $2800. The difference would be that cloth diapers are reusable for other future babies in the family to use.

Convenience

In the past with diapers, you would have to follow through complicated folds and scary pins, but nowadays, cloth diapers are made with buttons, snap closures and Velcro, making it just as easy to change a baby's dirty diapers as disposable ones. They have also come a long way from the white cloth used in earlier times. Cloth diapers now come in different cloths laced with baby friendly designs and colors, and also include waterproof bands around the legs and waist to avoid leaks. They are also able to absorb almost as much as disposable waste with their removable linings. Cloth diapers, though, more often require diaper changes, since they aren't as absorbent as disposable ones, so keep that in mind.

Which type of diaper best keeps diaper rash at bay?

Cloth diapers tend to be more comfortable and breathable, while they also do a great task as long as you can ensure you get it changed as quickly as it is soiled. Disposables allow for your baby to be kept comfortable and dry for longer periods because of their absorbing creams. The absorbent gels hold huge amount of fluids and can keep them away from your baby's skin. This means your baby's skin is kept dry longer, also minimizing skin contact with urine and even some parts of stool. There are also breathable disposable diapers with material that support air flow to your toddler's skin. Also, various disposable diaper brands now contain protective coating substances that keep the skin protected, like barrier creams the likes of Balmex do. However, some babies develop heat or skin rashes while wearing disposable diapers; it could be an allergic trigger, or the diaper being too tight. If this is the case, experiment with a distinct size or brand, or you can switch to traditional cloth diapers.

Making the decision

The right choice depends on what suits your family's needs and lifestyle. Development in production technology has improved the options available for both cloth and disposable diapers. Nothing stops you from using a combination of both, and other parents have actually done the same. For example, some use cloth diapers for newborns and younger babies, while using disposables for toddlers who are more active, or some use disposables during the night, so as not to interrupt sleep on wet diapers and cloth diapers during the day, or you could also decide to use cloth diapers at home and disposables when you're outside or travelling.

Cutting on costs

As the cost of diapers can be heavy, here are some tips to help get some savings:

Know how much your diapers cost

The first step to saving is to understand how much the cost is per diaper. This allows you to calculate and decide if a sale is great or not, or if you can couple it with coupons or other discounts for a good deal. This way, no matter what brands you choose, (considering price points or discounts tend to be higher for brands like Pampers compared to Luvs), you know what a good deal is for each brand and each size.

Buy in bulk!

Watch out for discount promos sales for buying bigger packs of diapers. They may not come too often, but you'll find that the cost per diaper tends to be lower (they also often come with a couple of free diaper pieces with larger packs). So, the bigger packs or boxes of diapers you buy the better.

Store branded diapers and wipes are just as good as expensive brands

The expensive brands are known for quality, but you'll find that store brands do just as well if not better. Savvy parents also make savings from mixing them up with branded disposable diapers. They use the cheapest in the daytime at home, and then use the more expensive ones during travel or at night time for sleep time.

Always check for quality, despite the cost. Some diapers may be cheaper but can only hold half as much fluid, so you end up using more diapers in a pack. In the long run, you end up spending more than you thought you saved. For wipes, generic brands aren't too different from branded ones; they also come in fragrance-free and hypo-allergenic types.

Use Amazon Mom

You can save 20% off diapers through an Amazon Mom's Membership with their Subscribe & Save subscription. In addition to this, you also get $1 to $3 e-coupons regularly. Amazon also offers price matching for Walmart items, as it's their biggest competitor. That and your 20% savings makes a very good deal! Apart from saving on diapers with your membership, you can also enjoy a 15% baby registry discount.

Prevent wasteful purchases

Wipes tend to dry out when not used, which also means you can't buy them in bulk, unlike with diapers. Soft-packed wipes are particularly the ones that dry out easier, even when sealed.

So, to avoid wasting your budget, buy wipes in plastic containers if you plan to buy in bulk. You can also save the plastic containers and refill them with soft-packed wipes. Also make sure to store unopened soft-packed whites in a closed space while you aren't using them.

If your stored wipes seem a little dry, you can easily get them moist again with a bit of warm water. It sounds simple and logical, but you'll be surprised at how many parents throw away their boxes of wipes just because they seemed a bit dry!

Foods for every stage

This chapter will go through a wide selection of healthy vegan recipes for your introductory feeding regimen. You can get very creative with how you approach this process. However, these are my recommended food choices for feeding toddlers through the specific stages and how to prepare them.

Note: Storing foods for later

After you've completed any of the following recipes, you can store them in a fridge for up to 2 days. If there is too much food and your baby will not finish it in 1 or 2 days, you can freeze the food in separate pieces. Place the food in an ice cube tray and freeze it. Next, remove the cubes and store in a gallon bag or container. Tag the bag/container accordingly and date and use anytime within three months.

4-6 Months

The introductory foods given to a baby are known as **stage 1** baby foods. They are mostly pureed or mashed, so your toddler can gulp them down effortlessly. However, there is no guarantee your baby will react well to any of the foods that follow these guidelines, so make sure to consult the opinion of a pediatrician prior to feeding any new food to your little one.

Peach, Pear and Apple Puree

Ingredients

1/3 cup peaches, skinned, cored and chopped

1 cup apples, peeled, seeded and chopped

1 cup pears, skinned, cored and chopped

2 tbsps. of water

Directions

Put chopped peaches, pears and apples in a cooking pan and add the water. Cook to a boil, then lower the heat until fruit is softened around 10 minutes. For a creamier consistency, puree with a potato masher.

Apple, Blueberry and Banana Puree

Ingredients

1 apple, skinned and diced

50 grams blueberries

1 tbsp. apple juice

1 ripe and spotted banana

Directions

Put the apple pieces in a saucepan and add in the apple juice. Cover for two minutes as it simmers. Next add the blueberries for another 2 minutes. Add the banana pieces and cook for one more minute. Remove the mixture and puree in a blender. Serve.

Potato and Zucchini Puree

Ingredients

2 cups zucchini, skinned and chopped

2 cups veggie broth

2 cups potatoes, skinned and diced

1 tbsp. olive oil

0.5 teaspoon salt

Directions

In a pot, set water on high and cook potatoes until soft. In a saucepan, sauté the chopped zucchini in olive oil and add the salt. Cover and let sit on medium heat until fully tender. Remove both potatoes and zucchini and puree them in a mixer as well as the veggie broth. Serve right away.

Roasted Pear Puree

Ingredients

3 regular pears

0.25 teaspoon cinnamon

0.5 teaspoon vanilla

Directions

Pre-heat oven to 400 F. Cut pears in halves and core the middle. Place pears bottom up in a non-stick baking pan. Transfer to oven and bake for 20 minutes. Take out to cool and skin, then add all ingredients into a blender and mix until a smooth consistency is reached. Serve immediately!

Apple Puree

Ingredients

1 apple

Water

Directions

Start by washing and peeling the apple and slice it into small chunks. Transfer the apple pieces to a pressure cooker. Add about 2-3 cups of water. Cook the apples in the pressure cooker for 2 whistles. Place the pressure cooker under running water to cool down.

After the apple chunks are well cooked, place them in a blender and mix to a puree, adding water to thin out the consistency.

Cauliflower and Broccoli Puree

Ingredients

1 head cauliflower

Preheat the steamer. In the meantime, rinse the cauliflower and broccoli and lay out as florets.

Move to steamer and steam for around 10 or 15 minutes, until fully tender.

Puree the broccoli and cauliflower separately, adding hot water to achieve a soft texture. Serve as is.

Plum and Beetroot Puree

Ingredients

2 red plums, cut in half and cored
2 beetroot, skinned and chopped into small cubes

Directions

Move the plums and beetroot into a saucepan and fill with water.

Let cook to a boil on high, then lower the heat, cover and simmer until the beetroot is tender, about 10-15 minutes.

Put the plums and beetroot in a mixer and blend until smooth.

Broccoli, Tahini and Pear Puree

Ingredients

2 pears
1 broccoli head
3 tbsp. tahini
Water

Directions

Preheat your steamer. Rinse the broccoli and spread into florets and transfer to steamer.

Skin and cut the pears into small pieces. Add to the steamer for around 10-15 minutes until food is tender.

After food is tender, transfer from heat and throw in the tahini and puree to desired consistency.

Let cool and serve.

Zucchini, Pea and Mint Puree

Ingredients

2 zucchini

Handful of peas

1 tbsp. of finely chopped mint leaves

Water

Directions

Fill a pot with water and cook over medium heat and put the steamer above it and cook to a boil.

Cut the zucchini into chunks and move to the steamer with the peas.

Dash with mint and cook until the zucchini is tender, for around 10-15 minutes.

Puree and add boiled water to achieve a smooth consistency.

Apple and Butternut Squash

Ingredients

2 red apples

1 butternut squash

Dash of cinnamon

Directions

Preheat oven to 170 degrees.

Chop the butternut squash in half and remove the seeds.

Place the squash cuts face up in a cooking pan.

Skin and slice the apples and put them inside the squash. Dash with cinnamon

Bake in oven until the flesh is soft and tender, around 40 minutes

Take out the apples and squash and puree well, thinning out with water. Serve.

6-9 months

Crockpot Applesauce

Ingredients

2 lbs. butternut squash, skinned, cored and diced

3 lbs. apples, skinned, cored and sliced

1/2 teaspoons granulated cinnamon (optional)

1/2 cups water

Directions

Note: Not all babies can tolerate spices before 12 months, so be careful if you are giving your baby spices for the first time.

Start by putting the squash and apples in the interior of the crockpot along with the nutmeg and cinnamon. Mix to a fine coat and fill in with ½ cups of water. Cover to cook for around 5 hours on medium heat. Once finished cooking, you can drain any of the excessive liquid. Finally, puree so the apple sauce is soft enough for your toddler.

Beets, blueberry and beats mash

Ingredients

2 Regular medium beets, cleaned well with water, skin and dice into chunks

S Cup frozen blueberries

Directions

Place the chopped/skinned beats into a saucepan with the blueberries. Fill with a sufficient water so it covers the top of the blueberries and beets and cook for 10-15 minutes on medium, until beets are softened. Transfer into a blender and mix until smooth. Serve immediately.

Blueberry, Avocado and Mango Raw Puree

Ingredients

S1/2 Cup blue berries

1 thick slice of mango, skinned and chopped

1 avocado

Directions

You can choose to puree with a fork until all fruit is gathered, so you get a chunky consistency, or you can toss the mixture into a blender for 20 seconds to get a smooth consistency.

As with most avocado purees, this recipe is ideal if consumed a little while after making it.

Peach-Mango Puree

Ingredients

1 Mango, cored, skinned and sliced into chunks

1 Peach, pitted and chopped

1 or 2 Tablespoons unsweetened breastmilk or water

1 or 2 Tablespoons any baby cereal

Directions

Mix peach, mango and liquid into a blender until consistency is soft. Add in cereal, or if your baby cannot tolerate thicker foods you can choose to not add cereal at all. Serve as is or refrigerate if preferred.

Pumpkin and Thyme Mash

Ingredients

1 Small Pumpkin

1-2S Cups Breast Milk or Water

1 Teaspoon fresh thyme

Directions

Preheat oven to 350 F. Put parchment paper over a baking sheet. Slice the top of the pumpkin, than cut in half from top to bottom, core out the middle until it's clean, but don't stress over removing the strings, as they will puree along with the pumpkin.

Dice the pumpkin into cubes and move to the baking sheet, make sure skins are fully removed. Bake for 50 minutes or until very tender. Remove from oven and let cool, once cool enough to handle. Put all ingredients into a blender and mix. If the consistency is not smooth enough, just add more water.

Serve as is or add to oatmeal, pancakes or any of the puree you see fit.

Pasta with Vegetables and Cheese Sauce

Ingredients

1 S cups dailya vegan grated cheese

1 S cups earth balance vegan butter

1 Tbsp Soy or Almond Milk

1 Tbsp Chopped Broccoli Florets

1 Cup Whole Flour

4 Cups Pasta

Directions

Cook pasta as the package advises. Chop broccoli florets into small chunks and steam I a pot until tender, around 10 minutes. In the meantime, in a skillet or saucepan, melt the vegan butter. Throw in the flour and stir well, gradually adding the vegan milk, stirring occasionally until the sauce is creamy. Add in the Daiya cheese and stir. Add the veggies and cooked pasta. Stir until gathered and serve hot or warm.

Pear and cinnamon oatmeal

Ingredients

1 cup oats

S cup soy milk

S cup water

1 pear, skinned, cored, grated dash of cinnamon

Directions

Place the oafs, milk and water in a pan and cook to simmer for around 5 minutes while constantly stirring. Remove mixture into a bowl and stir in the rest of the ingredients. Set aside to cool down and serve.

Potato, broccoli and pea puree

Ingredients

Black pepper

50g frozen peas

100g broccoli

Soy milk

Earth balance vegan butter

350g potatoes

Directions

Skin and dice potatoes, put the broccoli and the potatoes in a steaming basket for around 10 minutes.

Add in the peas at the last 3-4 minutes.

After all the veggies have tenderized, transfer to a bowl and puree well, adding seasoning and he vegan butter. Serve as is or with added breast milk, if you would prefer to thin this out for your baby.

9-12 months

Banana quinoa puree

Ingredients

S Ripe banana

Dash of cinnamon

3 Tablespoons quinoa

1 Tablespoon Daiya vegan yogurt

Directions

Put banana in a bowl and mash to puree. Throw in the remainder of the mix and stir in. Serve as is or refrigerate to cool.

Apple and apricot crumble

Ingredients

1-3 large sized apples

4-6 apricots, or S canned apricots

1 tablespoon cinnamon

3 tablespoons ground almond

30 grams organic sugar

50 grams Natures Balance vegan butter

150 grams white flour

Directions

Preheat oven to 220 F. Cut the apples into small pieces, then put in a skillet or saucepan, cover the apples with water and bring to a boil. Reduce the heat to a simmer and add cinnamon, stir often for 6 minutes or until the apples are tender. In the meantime, put the flour and vegan butter in a clean bowl and caress them until they have a flakey consistency, next add the sugar and stir.

Dice the apricots and core out the stones. Turn off the heat and stir in the apricot chunks, than transfer the mix into a baking dish. Layer with the crumble mixture and top off with crushed almonds. Put in the oven and cook for 30 minutes or until the top is golden brown coated. Set aside to cool before serving.

Tomato, carrot and cauliflower with basil

Ingredients

2 Medium carrots, skinned and chopped

2 Regular tomatoes, skinned, cored and finely diced

1 Cup cut cauliflower florets

2 Tablespoons unsalted vegan butter (any brand, vegan)

2-3 Basil leaves

S Cup grated Daiya vegan cheese

Directions

Put the carrots in a skillet or saucepan. Cover and add water and bring to a boil. Lower heat to a simmer and cook for 10 minutes, throw in the cauliflower florets and cover, cook for another 8 minutes. In the meantime melt the vegan butter in a separate pan, than throw in the tomatoes and cook on medium heat until mushy.

Remove the mixture and add in the vegan cheese and basil. Mash the cauliflower and carrots with the tomato sauce and about S cup of the leftover liquid.

Dried apricot puree

Ingredients

2 Cups any brand diced apricots

4 Cups all natural apple juice

Directions

Finely cut the fruit and mix with juice in a pan or skillet. Cook to a boil then lower the heat to simmer. Take mixture out of pan and let cool down before pureeing. Use water to puree to your desired consistency.

Sweet spinach

Ingredients

1 ripe banana

2-3 cups spinach

Directions

Fill pot with to around 1 inch depth and boil over medium heat.

Transfer spinach into a floating steamer basket and boil the basket in a pot, not letting the water contact the spinach.

Cover the pot and let simmer for around 6 minutes and mix until consistency is creamy and serve immediately.

Yogurt and beat puree

Ingredients

1 beet

2 cups any vegan variety milk and plain daiya yogurt.

Directions

Cut off the stems from the beats, rinse beats off using cold faucet water, skin and chop.

Fill a pot with water until about 2 inches are covered and cook to a boil.

Put beets in a mixer of your choice and puree until consistency is smooth. Set aside to cool and serve with yogurt topping.

Black beans with zuccini and corn

Ingredients

1/2 can of black beans, rinsed and drained

1 zuccini, rinsed and sliced

1 cup fresh or frozen corn

Directions

Pour around 1 inch of water into a pot and bring to a boil. Transfer the zuccini and corn into a floating steamer basket and transfer into the boiling pot, making sure the water does not have contact with the basket. Cover the pot and let simmer for 7 minutes.

Next place the zuccini and corn into a blender along with the black beans and mix until consistency is thick and chunky, but just soft enough that the baby can ingest with ease.

Muesli breakfast

Ingredients

15g oats

3/4 cup soy milk

5 dry apricots, softened in warm water

1 pear, skinned and chopped

Directions

Put oats and soy milk in a cooking pan, cook to a simmer for around 3 minutes until the puree is thick. Let cool and put in a mixer with the boiled apricots and chopped pears. Blend well until consistency is creamy and smooth

Mixed fruit muesli

Ingredients

1 tablespoon raisin

1 pear

1 hand full chopped raisins

Directions

Put the oats and milk in a bowl and soak overnight, skin the pear and grate it into the rest of the mixture. Stir in the raspberries and raisins and serve.

Rice pudding

Ingredients

S cup soy or breast milk

3 tablespoons rice

2 drops vanilla essence

Directions

Put the milk in a pan and heat until hot. Add in the rice and mix until the consistency is creamy and free of lumps. Turn off the heat and add in the vanilla and mix. Serve as is.

Mini pancakes with berry yogurt

Ingredients

1s cup white flour

1 whole vegan egg replacer (any brand)

2/3 cups soy milk

1 tablespoon olive oil

1//4 cup daiya yogurt

1 fresh strawberry

2 fresh blueberries

2 fresh raspberries

Directions

Pour flour in a bowl. Add the milk and egg and whisk until batter mix is smooth. Next cook the oil over mid heat, stirring occasionally so the butter does not stick. Add a spoon of two of the mix for about 1 minute, flip over to the other side and cook for half an hour. Finally mix the fruit with the yogurt and blend well.

Banana Dosa

Ingredients

1/2 cup mashed banana

1/2 cup dosa batter

1 or 2 teaspoon sugar

Earth balance vegan butter

1 teaspoon of date syrup

Preparation

Condition the spoons and bowls for your toddler in a compartment with hot water for 5 minutes and keep them there until use.

Directions

Mash bananas with a fork or your hand. Mix the dosa in with the bananas until texture is smooth. Set aside.

Heat up a skillet and add a small portion of banana dose batter and even it out to make a mini dosa, add a hint of the butter or oil. Cook on one side until brown, around 5 minutes. Let cook for another minute and take off of heat. Do the same for the rest of the mix.

Apple, parsnip and carrot mash

Ingredients

4 carrots

4 parsnips

4 apples

Dash of cinnamon

1 tablespoon olive oil

Directions

Skin and chop carrots, apples and parsnips and move them to a salad bowl with a dash of cinnamon and olive oil. Stir in well.

Transfer the mixture from bowl into a baking pan with some slight oil and cook at 400 degrees for around 25 minutes until foods are tender to a fork touch. Once done baking, set aside to cool and mash as needed.

Lentil, apple and sweet potato salad

Ingredients

3 medium sized sweet potatoes

1 regular sized apple

2 cups tablespoon olive oil

1 teaspoon cinnamon

Directions

Skin the sweet potatoes and chop into small cubes, skin core and chop the apple into small chunks. Add lentils and 2 cups of the broth or water to a boil in a pot. Lower the heat once the lentils start boiling. Continue to cook lentils on low heat for about 25 min until lentils have softened.

Add 1 cup of water to a separate cooking pot as well as in steam basket into it.

Add the diced apple and sweet potato chunks to the steaming basket and simmer for around 20 minutes, until sweet potatoes are softened.

After the sweet potatoes and lentils are cooked, move to a sink and drain any excess juice from the saucepots. Allow to warm.

After foods have warmed, mix the foods in a salad bowl with 2 tablespoons of olive oil. Add a dash of the spices and stir well.

Peachy sweet potatoes

Ingredients

1 sweet potato, skinned and chopped

2 fresh potatoes, cored and chopped

Dash of cinnamon ginger

Water

Directions

Merge peaches and sweet potatoes in a cooking tray with enough water to just cover the food. Garnish with a dash of cinnamon and stir. Cover the dish with foil. Cook for around 20 minutes until sweet potatoes and peaches are tender.

After fully cooked, save any left over water and move peaches and sweet potatoes to a bowl to cool. Puree to your babies desired preference and serve.

Final Words

Raising a vegan baby is very rewarding although it calls for efficiency and dedication. If you are a first time parent it may also be too overwhelming because there is not much time to learn from past mistakes when bringing up a baby, but I truly hope the information in this book has helped you overcome many of these hurdles.

Thank you for reading! If you enjoyed my book and would recommend it to anyone. I'd be very grateful if you can leave a short review on Amazon. Your feedback is really important and I will use the opportunity to find out how I can improve this book even more.

Thanks again for your support!

Made in the USA
Middletown, DE
05 May 2020

93653208R00052